ANTIQUE TOOLS...

OUR AMERICAN HERITAGE

By Kathryn McNerney

Photography: Tom McNerney

COLLECTOR BOOKS
A Division of Schroeder Publishing Co., Inc.

**FOR MY SON TOM L.
AND
MY 'BIG BROTHER' ARNOLD**

*To share with the Mister
who collects old American
tools and the Missus who
buys many of them for him.*

The current values in this book should be used only as a guide. They are not intended to set prices, which vary from one section of the country to another. Auction prices as well as dealer prices vary greatly and are affected by condition as well as demand. Neither the Author nor the Publisher assumes responsibility for any losses that might be incurred as a result of consulting this guide.

Additional copies of this book may be ordered from:

COLLECTOR BOOKS
P.O. Box 3009
Paducah, Kentucky 42002-3009

@$9.95. Add $2.00 for postage and handling.

Printed by IMAGE GRAPHICS, INC., Paducah, Kentucky

CONTENTS

ON THE COVER

FRONT :

    Plane ....$75.00–125.00.

    Hand cornsheller ....$25.00.

    Loggers iron ....$42.50.

    Cobbler's rasp ....$22.50.

    Level ....$69.00.

    Drawknives ....$35.00–38.00 (ea)+.

    Buggy wrench ....$22.50–25.00.

    Broadaxe ....$125.00 variable.

    Tobacco stakes frow ....$45.00 variable.

    Devil tool (railroad) ....$40.00.

BACK:

    Cannonball tongs (Civil War) ....$95.00.

    Crosscut saw ....$55.00.

    Coopers drawshave ....$75.00.

    Surveyor's wheel ....$125.00+.

    Entrenching tool (Civil War) ....$125.00.

    Corner chisel ....$95.00+.

3

APPRECIATION

While gathering materials I kept asking questions, gratefully jotting down in my faithful blue notebook bits and pieces of opinions and facts volunteered by folks who saw us with camera and tripod at shows but who quietly left without identifying themselves.

The subject of the old American tools just keeps going, but since this book must be closed somewhere — the time has come to offer a heartfelt THANK YOU to all the collectors, dealers, and personnel of several historical and working museums and restorations and private business organizations, such as the Jack Daniels Distillery at Lynchburg, Tennessee. To the producers of the Cox Hoosier Antiques Exposition and the Crutcher Antiques Show and Sale who permitted photography at Indianapolis, Indiana, each was kindly interested and cooperative.

Of invaluable help were John Brown's Antiques, Florida; The Harlow Autreys' Olden Days, the George and Steven Fellows families, Georgia; the Joe Harrods, Kinnetts Antiques, The Red Door, and Pioneer Village at Spring Mill State Park, Mitchell, all in Indiana; Betty and Lloyd Allen's Russellville Antique Mall, Concord Antiques, the Robert Douglas family, Gyp Joint, Albert Holeman, Lee's Flea Market, Jane Macomber, The Hitching Post, and Tennessee Valley Authority's Land Between the Lakes Iron Furnace, Empire Farm and Educational Center and The Homeplace — 1850 (western Kentucky and Tennessee), in Kentucky; Virginia Clark, Massachusetts; the Charles James' and Ray Bonneau's Pontiac Shoppe of Antiquity and Newman & Chase, Michigan; Chase's Collectors' Corner, New York; Mountain Laurel Antiques, North Carolina; Charles Hodges, Robert Leath, and Mearl Ward, Ohio; Murfreesboro's Cannonburgh Restoration and Larry and Taney Sim's Murfreesboro Antique Mall, both in Tennessee.

❖❖❖❖❖❖❖❖❖❖

DATES and VALUES

Since few old American tools carry completion or patent dates, to learn something of their origins inspect imprinting or embossing with a magnifying glass (I once found a rough mallet with the owner's name his faint 'X' knifecut into the handle); note acknowledged regional and group typical styles (Pennsylvania Dutch, Zoar, Amish, Shaker, New England, Western, etc.); talk with the owners if possible; look for similars; and pursue whatever other evidence seems relevant.

Unless the maker did, luckily, mark them, tools herein are intended as circa, meaning about or around the time of, such as circa: 1776. They are also to be regarded as handcut or handcarved in woods, handtooled in leathers, and handforged or wrought in metals unless identified with (F) for factory made.

It was habitual for early employers such as Wells Fargo, circuses, railroads, and river and ocean lines to hire their own carpenters, black-smith/farriers, and coopers. And just as those skilled workers marked their own tools against misplacement and theft, so did the companies. Further, a century and more ago for a tool to be factory made could be interpreted as containing a certain amount of handwork as opposed to our present customary machine-totality.

At first, rising more slowly than numerous other collectables, tool prices are now escalating even more rapidly. Increasing numbers of buyers are steadily depleting the still fairly good supply of old tools left around. Mounting interest is also apparent from the growth of active members in old tool clubs throughout our country.

Values of the more plentiful average tools (so-called from compara-ble appearance, condition, abundance, and better known crafts special-ization groups) are somewhat predictable. But especially at auctions the prices of the scarce exotics (the skillfully formed, touchmarked, one-of-a-kind) are amazingly unpredictable. Geographic fluctuations in economy; proximity to the original source where an artifact gains con-siderably in importance (and price) because of local interest; travel sub-ject to seasonal weather hazards; accommodations affecting which markets and how many can be visited according to preplanned trip time and expense budgets; transportation costs if something needs com-mercial moving (as a farmwagon or loom); stability and completeness of an item and whether a workable substitute for a missing or broken part can be contrived or purchased are all big factors in buying.

We have tried to present many rare and expensively glamorous old tools as well as others with practical and/or historical appeal which are less costly but equally fascinating for all purses.

Prices shown were sales-tagged by reputable dealers. In reporting them we cannot be responsible for inaccuracies; none are personal opin-ions nor estimates. They are simply value guides and not meant to be inflexible.

Pieces in private ownership are priced according to similar pieces viewed elsewhere.

Taking that first tentative step in browsing among the tools with which our forebears 'made out' can easily lead to an expanding interest in even more thought-provoking jaunts.

THE ENDURING TOOLS

The blacksmith of an early settlement eased his considerable bulk into a sagging rocker, lifted his coarsely-woven-socked feet onto another, and groaned in pure contentment. Full as a tick after fried meat and potatoes, he reached behind one ear for a pick he'd whittled from kindlin' and carefully probed for stray slivers of supper. His missus shuffled to the open scarred plank door, drying her knuckley red hands on a long mealsack apron. She leaned against the jamb hoping for a breath of cooler air, fanning and mopping her sweatstreaked face with the same cloth. "I orter git on over t' th' store fer a slab a' bacon but m' limbs is plumb wored out." Idly slapping mosquitoes the man grunted agreeably, "So'm I; if'n a mule wuz t' set down on me right now I wouldn' even try t' git up." He drawled on, "Soon bedtime; got a plow t' sharpen kum sunup." Yet he lingered, pondering again on his Pa's coming so far from the ocean coast to build the first forge here 'longside his two-crib (rooms) dogtrot (open center passage-way) cabin not far from an iron furnace.

FORGE and Forge Tools, $7.00–35.00. (F)

CENTER FURNACE, 1840. Established at former Hematite, KY. "Give'er fire!"

He had lived off the land carrying only two tools, a knife in its sheath and a shorthaft axe handle stuck under his belt, which Pa treated every bit as good as his rifle and his horse.

And when he couldn't do another lick a' work Pa turned over the whole shebang, advising him to "later do th' same fer his'n; take plenty of time on a job of repairing old and making new tools t' last from the best materials available; protect them from weathering and damage by using special box (later tool chest) for handily moving about all together; never loan any!"

PINE TOOLCHEST, $78.00.

8

Now, as in the beginning, tools created by man are used by him to further create, visual immortal expressions of man's remarkable imagination and invincible determination.

He watched other creatures converting natural elements to their particular needs; hornets chewed twigs and leaves for a sticky secretion binding their hanging nests; another wasp species rolled tiny flat stones to smooth the earth disturbed over its newly laid eggs. Imitating

in his own way, man started picking up eoliths lying on the ground (they the simple stones, the earliest known tools in our assumed culture of man), using the sharper edge for scraping and the heavier to bring down moving and slay sleeping animals. Responding to endowed ingenuity and vaguely-felt but so slowly emerging ideas of even better ways to get along, man sensed he must not only reach out beyond his physical limitations for accomplishment by merely using the stones, but that he must strive to improve them in both form and application to pace his expanding thoughts.

Thus for hundreds of thousands of years man awkwardly piled stones for shelters, tried flaking and smashing them together to gain added food, protection, and coverings, fashioned them into less violently inclined implements for primitive agriculture, and as civilization advanced, used them for games. And so tools gave man directional control of his continuing progression.

The TRADE AXE was bartered with the Indians by the early settlers, the first probably fashioned by a frontier smith, the second more resembling a type that might have been carried by French fur trappers and traders. These were not only weapons but could have been peacefully used for axes by the Indians as were their tomahawks when not making war.

AXE, $75.00.

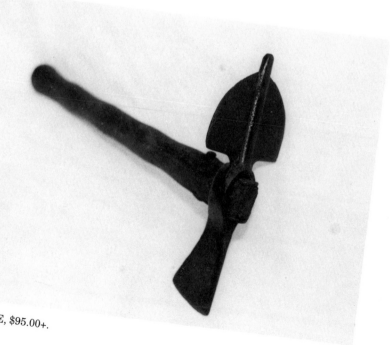

AXE TRADE, $95.00+.

Many designed their own tools. A blacksmith concentrated on strong keen blades, wood parts left to the carpenter or customer. Families might design their own hatchets or axe handles, for which they and their locale became widely recognized; copies were regarded as forgeries. At completion of a tool the woodworker might pridefully, plainly cut or intricately carve his touchmark, such as initials, dot designs, flowers, or a rare date, this last simplifying research.

The smith impressed his mark in hot iron with nails and punches; the tinner, if he marked at all, seemed to prefer dates.

GOOSEWING BROADAXE, similar to shapes found at the site of seventeenth century Jamestown, Virginia. $550.00+.

The farrier, a smith who also shod animals, known to have practiced his craft in 500 B.C. Greek culture, usually had some practical knowledge of veterinarian skills essential in a society of land animal strength. This was doubly imperative on remote cavalry posts and in early settlements, which often staked out and held as free land a central plot to entice such a craftsman.

11

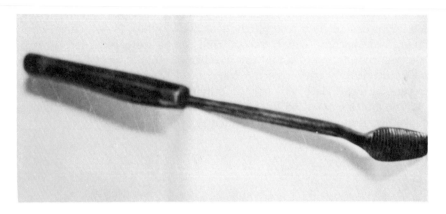

FARRIERS' FLOAT (Horsetooth Rasp). $35.00.

Livery Stables — board and stalls plus rentals of horses and 'rigs' — mostly owned and operated by a farrier with one helper, grew separately from earlier ordinaries (hostels) until after the turn of the 1900's. They declined under community objections to their clouds of huge horseflies and their problems of accumulated wastes in a growing new awareness of health and sanitation hazards.

Horse conveyances of people and goods were also being steadily eroded by such group transportation as trolley and interurban (traction) lines and railroads.

SIGN, painted heavy paper. $50.00.

12 POUNDER — CIVIL WAR CANNON, World War II closed the era of colorful horse soldiers and destructively impressive horsedrawn field artillery.

LIMBER, this carried powder and cannonballs and had a 2-cannoneers' seat. A four-horse team for short and a six-horse team for long distances was hitched to the limber which in turn hauled the cannon backwards.

The following depict a few of the innumerable contributing accessories that were the essential backgrounds maintaining the arenas in which handtools could be manually applied, all factory made.

Kerosene LANTERN from a line once operating only from Nashville to Franklin, Tennessee. $95.00.

Kerosene clear globe BRAKEMAN'S HAND-LANTERN, $55.00.

Red and green ribbed glass railroad SIGNAL LAMP, kerosene. $135.00.

RAILROAD TORCH to thaw impacted ice and snow from switch locks; tinned iron; kerosene burned through a waste cotton wick protected by a 1" high collar; handle; both wick and filler openings have chained caps; note edge beading. $55.00.

INSULATOR, 1800's, wood, iron ends. One end attached to a supporting pole, the other to an overhead trolley wire insulated electricity from the ground; used on traction lines, our first streetcars, and finally on electrified railroads, later replaced by ceramic parts. Present electrified mass transportation uses a third rail since overhead wires exposed to the elements would be too costly to maintain. $9.50.

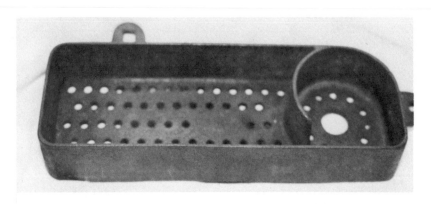

FIELD IMPLEMENT
TOOLCARRIER, $22.50.

LIFE PRESERVER, canvas
stitched on cork, saltspray
cracked. $95.00.

BELAYING PIN, carved from
one piece green oak; fit into
deckside slot for wrapping
ropes; sometimes forcibly
applied on seamen for rough
discipline a long time ago.
$45.00.

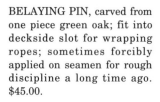

16

Paddlewheel steamers briefly commercially held on. Today we have extensively improved towboat-barge shipping on our principal lakes and rivers with several passenger stern paddlewheelers such as The Delta and Mississippi Queens still faithfully and luxuriously plying Ol' Man River and several tributaries.

WOOD PADDLEWHEEL

STEAMBOATS' ENGINEERS' WRENCH, $55.00. (F)

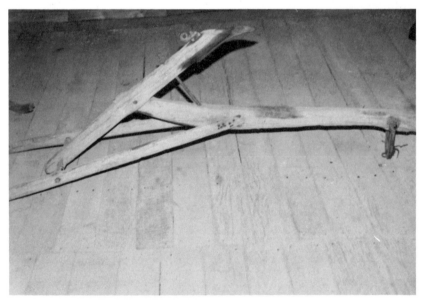

Smith's duties had always been heavy but now they dominated as homesteaders settled even more farms, plantations, and ranches, and towns boomed around 1890. Forges rarely cooled, turning out endless irons for building, housekeeping, new plowshares, and other tilling implements, most needing constant sharpening and repairs. Shown are two SINGLE BLADE PLOWS, crude but sharply effective; one has natural branch handles easily replaceable, man-pushed, mule-pulled.

Our blacksmith drowsily contemplating his hardearned financial independence could not imagine how relatively short would be his type of individual career security as earthtime is measured. A farrier could manage a basic income as long as shod animals participated in man's labor or recreational activities but a smith's work as first practiced might one day become legendary.

It is interesting that in the latter 1700's and throughout the 1800's, with some inheritances still intact into the earlier 1900's, many craftsmen, particularly in smaller towns, owned a parcel of land within a reasonable distance where cultivation of crops, flocks, and/or herds assured an income when their regular trades were slow.

Holstein Oxen

Others apprenticed and then adopted a second occupation, supplying themselves with the extra tools, to keep working full-time during seasonal fluctuations.

Families could usually grow enough food for their own consumption but in the struggle of homesteading during the 1700's and earliest 1800's the sale of wood became a welcome source of cash.

With orders for white pine (flexible straight grain wood without knots) masts and spars increasing here and abroad, and with those trees abundant in many areas, it was no problem to log them, floating them as rafts on the rivers to sawmills and ports.

We didn't originate tools; they were carried here by our forefathers,

19

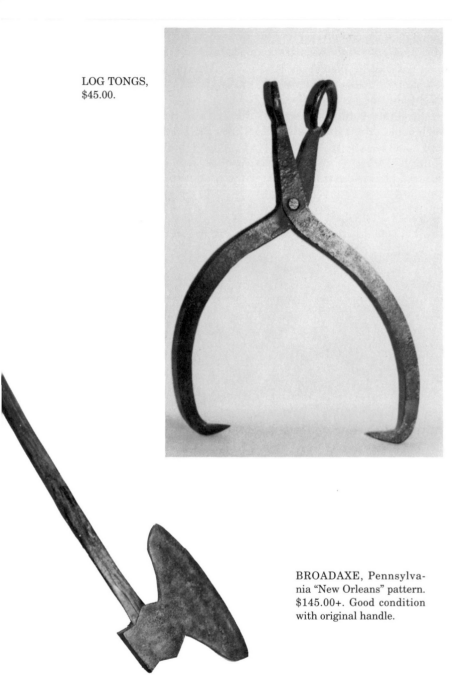

LOG TONGS, $45.00.

BROADAXE, Pennsylvania "New Orleans" pattern. $145.00+. Good condition with original handle.

who improved them to their needs and notions, with new ones added from designs recalled from those once familiarly applied in other lands.

For the settlers a large variety of tools was superfluous and not readily obtainable anyway. The axe, our first construction tool, had to do just about everything from felling, cutting, chopping, and trimming, to making basic cabinware. (Touchmarks on axes were not uncommon, dates were.)

The chisel edge broadaxe squared logs into beams, a type of striking plane. In the eighteenth century, with American practicality, craftsmen devised a steel band about 1½" wide forged onto the cutting base of the broadaxe for more strength and endurance, also adding a heavy poll to expedite chopping although it must have often supplied a convenient albeit awkward hammer, (not good for the metal).

Other earliest building tools were the auger, froe mallet and froe, corner and mortising chisels, broad slick and scoring adze, the last scoring marks on exposed decorative beams for broadaxe work, among other projects. The inside bevels of our earliest adzes were whetstone sharpened; later removable handles permitted using grindstones.

CARPENTERS' ADZE, $75.00.

In construction the mortise was the cavity, more commonly squared, into which a tenon was cut to fit. There were, however, other styles including the axe-pointed timber cornering, saddle notching rounded with the gutter adze, and in the earliest settlements a giant dovetailing cut with a lip adze. This last resembling the way nature

21

designed her doves' tails, surfaces slanting downward, which facilitated drainage and so closely locked the timbers together that only light chinking was necessary.

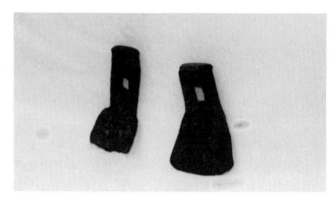

Two GUTTER ADZES for small special purposes. $22.00 each.

Aside from mortise cutting both the gutter and lip adze scooped out log drains, shown at this restoration.

Even though many early buildings here were held together with only mortise and tenon joints, nails were still needed for parts such as trim, clapboards, and shingles. We've all read that during Colonial times nails were so precious people moving on often burned down their homes to salvage those fasteners. This forced an act by the Virginia Legislature about 1645, that when a home was abandoned, if the owners did not burn it down, they would be compensated by receiving the approximate number of nails therein. Also, particularly in our northeastern regions, nail making might become a family enterprise when an iron deposit was discovered on their land, surplus nails sold to neighbors not so fortunate.

Where applicable, handcut wood pins, however, were invariably preferred over iron nails. These treenails (trunnels) were driven in with a wood mallet or burl hammer. Trunnels held better than iron, atmospheric humidity causing the tightly fitting pins to swell, holding a structure even more securely; nor did they rust, causing beams to rot.

CARPENTERS' BURL HAMMER, $68.00.

The resistant differences in the abnormal and the normal hardwoods consistently striking other objects is emphasized between the burl hammer and this heavily wear-damaged hickory carpenter's mallet. Burl, a rockhard knot to the Indians, or knurl to American pioneers is an abnormal diseased outgrowth seen on many trees, highly prized by early woodworkers during several centuries, but often too porous for practical usages. Ash, maple, and walnut, these of less porous quality, are found in tools and bowls, walnut only occasionally in bowls but prominently for inlays and veneers (Burled Walnut).

This magnificent burl was seen clinging desperately to a tree being felled along a busy highway. Notable for a protruding warty bulk in its natural environment the handsomely rare cut-exposed grain of the burl in its final usage can never afterwards be mistaken.

It is readily apparent which tool came from the clever hands of a craftsman with that indefinable knack and which one was laboriously contrived by another serious but simply dogged

CARPENTERS' MALLET, $8.50.

24

FARM IMPLEMENT
PART, $14.50.

FINGERHOLD NUT,
$10.00.

worker. But all
tools do extend our
abilities to grasp
and hold, cut, tight-
en, or measure.

These are good
examples of skillful
smithing in a
curled fingerhold
nut and a special
part for an early
farm implement.

The crudely
handcut but effi-
cient traveler (mea-
suring wheel) has a
deliberate nick on
one edge just above
center for eye
counting the revo-
lutions.

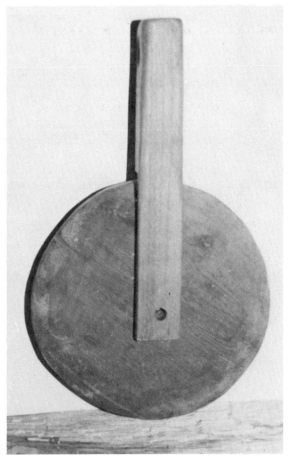

TRAVELER, $68.00.

Archeologists have unearthed Roman metal tongs, planes, bill hooks (in our case for pruning, in theirs, military), and chisels much like ours. Ancient drawings reveal Egyptians had similar saws.

Before American iron, and finally steel saws were developed, for over a hundred thousand years they were of stone, flint (which was a very hard, unyielding quartz), and bronze, all fairly inadequate. Blacksmiths here occasionally made them of these materials well into the 1800's, but most were European.

Until the early 1500's carpenters built only wood structures; it naturally followed that men with inherent aptitudes would try new ideas. So from these branched other specialists quickly adept in other areas such as finishing and carving. Turners were important for making rails and bedposts, any piece that could be wood lathe turned. Wheelwrights and coach makers developed as specialists with the progression of wagons and carriages. Previously the smith had included such pieces with his regular ironworking.

Stairmakers built stairs and carvers added beautiful embellishments to chairs, beds, paneling, and cabinets along with purely standard touches. Each craft experienced its own diversified expansion of skills, keeping up with our industrial strides. Patternmakers appeared with the building of more and more iron and brass foundries, making wooden patterns for objects to be cast in sand brass or iron poured into a sand mold. And each craft soon developed its own special tools.

Vastly used in the 1700's, wood continued in an even greater variety into the latter 1800's, so woodworkers financially 'did right well'.

(During those years almost every male old enough to hold a knife was, or aspired to be, a firstclass whittler, at home or seated with neighbors around a glowing coal or woodstove on wintry evenings, competitively comparing blades, measuring unbroken lengths of apple parings and shavings curls, 'gassin' about crops and politics, and dipping splendidly into the convenient cracker barrel of a country store.)

27

COAL BUCKET and SCUTTLE, $30.00 set. (F)

WOOD BARRELS, lapped-over hoops. $85.00+ each.

Sharing the convictions of earlier craftsmen — that which works good should be let alone — and although tools matured and multiplied at the side of man as our lives moved ahead, there were overall scarcely noted changes on innumerable originals for many generations. (One example, along with a great many wood planes, is the Artillery Gunner's Quadrant, the tool which set the bore of their cannon for different ranges, almost the same as that being now used—on the same principle.) And tools today directly encompass countless pursuits including extended research and interplanetary exploration, indirectly influencing all other areas of our existence. When in 1861 rose the sudden frantic rush for immediate war commodities, Dragons of Demand literally devoured a lot of the personal integrity and individual interest that lead to the superior quality products strictly instilled by the Guilds during the Middle Ages, chomping everything relentlessly into mass production. Where heretofore tools had generally meant manually used handtools (with implements), it gradually embraced as tools of trade whatever contributed to the result of an effort, such as my desk, this paper, advertising, even shipping and containers; but herein we are most concerned with the earlier definition.

(Still, most of us enjoy, and would dislike giving up, our favorite specialty items and longer vacations this modern efficiency has bestowed on us by entirely reverting to the slower rhythms and restric-

BURLEY TOBACCO CUTTER, $45.00.

tions of the often proclaimed good old days. However, there more and more seems to be a steadily upsurging trend toward interest in nostalgia that could evolve into a healthy combination of the best of both eras.)

Tools, starting from the same patterns, appeared in final forms from personal ideas for changes, individual requirements, and materials at hand. So when we find one we almost or exactly recognize but hear it called something different, then years of a regional habit or distortion of the original spelling and/or pronounciation have undoubtedly occurred.

A sturdy old 'assist' might be artfully-lovely or innocently-rough but we do know it was made with sincerity of workmanship, that someone held it respectfully in his hands to wield and cherish.

Turning on into this forest of pages of old American tools, recalling that each tool was first part of a woodlands tree or a deposit of raw metal in the earth, may you browse at your own pace the meandering trails, happily returning again and again.

BLACKSMITHS, FARRIERS, WHEELWRIGHTS

Early smiths were also wheelwrights. An ironworker was needed wherever humans gathered together on land; at sea they made harpoons on whalers and armament on men-of-war. Anvils are spoken of in the 700's B.C., and all were imported into America until c. 1845 when we began to manufacture them of much better quality using steel facings. There was considerable variety in sizes and forms such as single or double BEAK (Horn), GENERAL SMITHING, CONCAVE for bending metal strakes (tire rounds), and the FARRIER'S ANVIL with a full horn to balance shoes and two holes that held the PRITCHEL or blunt-nose punch hit with a hammer to put nailholes in horseshoes.

ANVIL VISE, quickly at hand when needed in forming hot iron. $75.00. (F)

ANVIL with solid log base hoopwrapped against splitting. $95.00. (F)
BALL PEEN HAMMER, $25.00. (F)
HOT and COLD CHISELS, $10.00+. (F)

ANVIL, $125.00. (F)
With hardy hole at end for ANVIL TOOLS that had to loosely fit for easy removal
(fullers, swages, bending and heading flatters). $22.00 (ea) var. (F)

STAKE ANVIL, set on anvil for light work as sheetmetal. $100.00. (F)

QUENCHING & TEMPERING TUB, iron banded oak, usually made by smith himself; kept near anvil to douse redhot irons and cool tongs to avoid burn-scarring jaws; smith could gauge tempering time; habitual top sooty scum.

LEATHER APRON, $35.00.
SWAGE HAMMER, $29.00. (F)

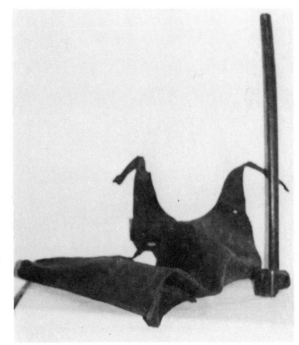

CARRIAGE IRONER'S
DOUBLE FACE
HAMMER, $45.00.

LEATHER APRON, $40.00.

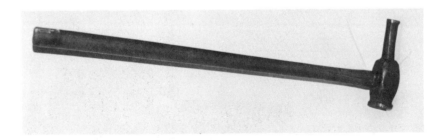

SMITH'S PUNCH, to start the driving out of pins. $35.00.
Light strong straight grained hickory was the preferred wood for hammer handles.

Uncommon CANNON-BALL TONGS from a cannonball factory that once was thriving in Pennsylvania during the Civil War; very large and heavy iron; cannonballs (as this 12 lb. solid shot) were to cause holes below the waterline and with tearing down the sails and rigging cause ships to sink; on land the same solidshots destroyed buildings. $95.00.

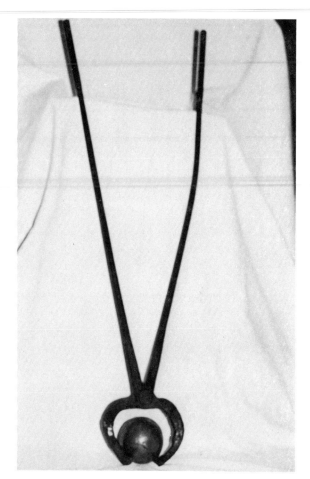

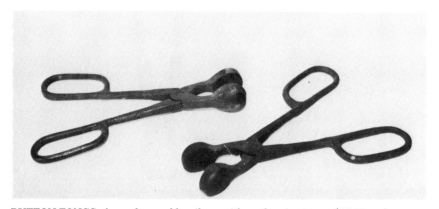

BUTTON TONGS, these also used by silversmiths as brazing tongs. $35.00 each.

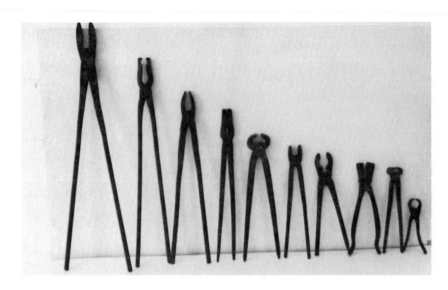

BLACKSMITH TONGS & PINCERS, farrier used some of them. $12.50+.
FLAT BIT, EYE or HAMMER, CUP JAWED, OVAL HOLDING, PICKUP
CLINCHER, and PINCERS TONGS.

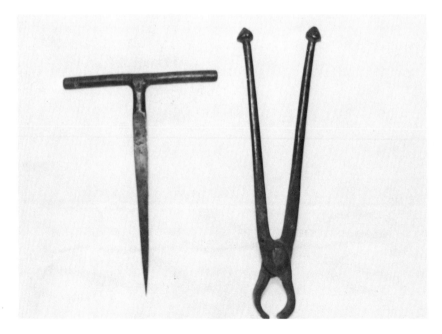

BURN AUGER, point was fired redhot in forge for penetrating wood, then twisted for
necessary size of hole. $28.00.
PINCER TONGS, buttons allowed a firmer grip; picked up heavier round irons. $35.00.

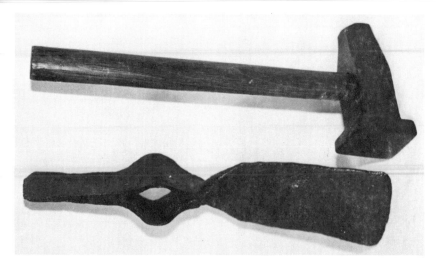

Smith's FLATTER, (smoothing). Hardened steel face. $29.00. (F)
A two-head finely handforged GRUBBING AXE evolved from the early hatchet-adze, mid-1800's. $38.00.

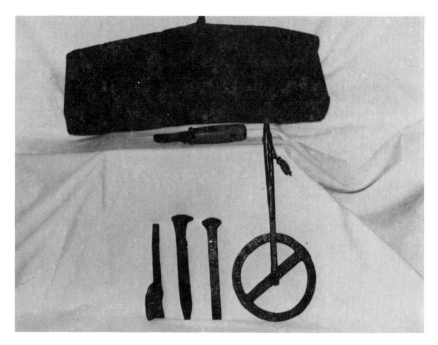

FARRIER'S NAILBOX, wood, metal base and handle. $45.00.
HOOFTRIMMER, $18.00.   SOLE KNIFE, $20.00.
NAILS, from a ship's flooring. $3.00 var.
TRAVELER, eighteenth century, measured tire after first measuring wheel it must fit. $125.00.

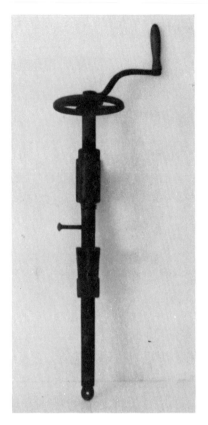

MANDREL, hollow cone for final shaping of rounds as hoops and hub bands; earliest were job-sized marked with erasable soapstone; mostly seen in restorations and museums. (Rare, expensive) $225.00+. (F)

BENCH DRILL, for metal boring using metal bits. $55.00. (F)

HACKSAW, iron. Brass collar on wood handle; cut iron as easily as saws cut wood. $68.00.

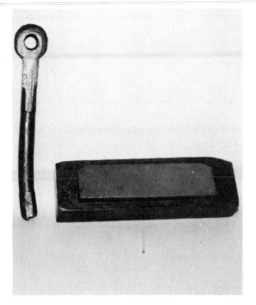

HORSESHOES WOODEN CALK REMOVER, factory stamped; eye to hang. $20.00.

BOLTHEADER, once so extensively in supply, bolt and nailheaders are not now easy to find. $46.00.
SMITH'S OILSTONE in a walnut box. $70.00.

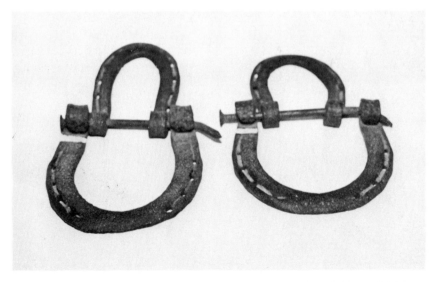

Two pairs of discarded HORSESHOES converted into CABIN HINGES with brief forge bending for the spikes; these the smith/farrier could supply, often by bartering, to ready-cash-scarce homesteaders. $45.00 pair.

SHOEING STAND, farrier made it from naturally curved hickory branch with third leg slashpegged into it; iron cap; to rest hoof during shoeing. $65.00.

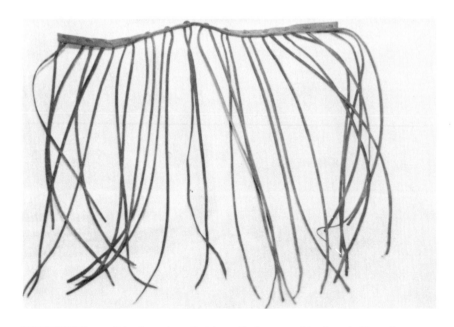

FLYSWITCH, small leather piece that in entirety covered back and sides of horse/mule. $28.00 for piece.

BUTTERIS, 1870. $75.00+.
MUDSHOE, wood, now obsolete, iron clamps held at hooftop around fetlock; snowbelt farm and logging usage on principle of snowshoes. $70.00.

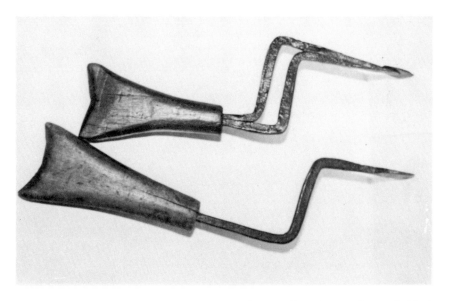

BUTTERIS, shoulder pressure used to trim hoof before adding shoe; made to individual order from basic pattern, rarely two identical. $75.00 (ea) var.

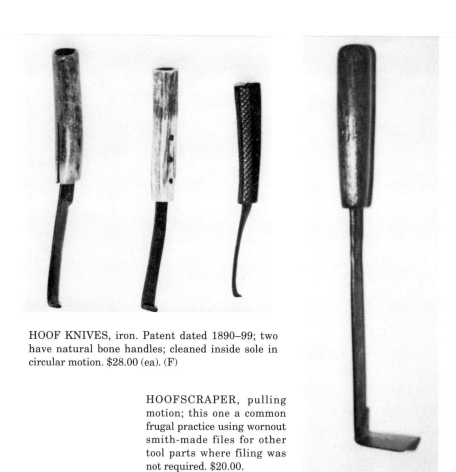

HOOF KNIVES, iron. Patent dated 1890–99; two have natural bone handles; cleaned inside sole in circular motion. $28.00 (ea). (F)

HOOFSCRAPER, pulling motion; this one a common frugal practice using wornout smith-made files for other tool parts where filing was not required. $20.00.

HOOFRASP, knob for second handhold. $12.50.

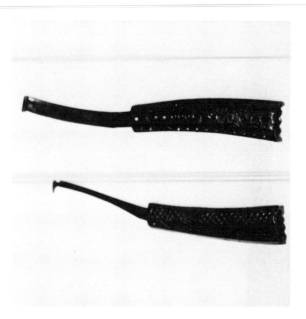

HOOF KNIVES, top: 'HELLER' with impressed horse outline, $35.00; bottom: 'E.J. POPE, Patd. 1899.' $28.00.

DOUBLE END HOOF RASP, sides slant oppositely from center; in picking it up farrier need not turn to use. $17.00 each. (F)

TANGED HOOF RASP, rough side here up was used first and finer, other side smoothed. $17.00.
CURRY COMB, both. $19.00. (F)

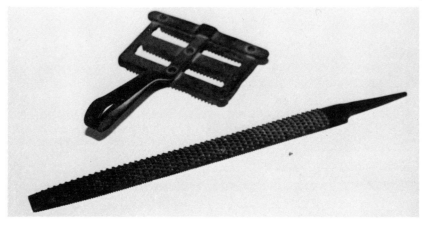

These WHEELWRIGHTS FELLOES
(Fellys), with broken pieces of spoke
ends in those holes, were dowel-
pinned at each end ready for tires
and the wheel spokes that held them
together. No price.

SPOKE ROUNDER,
$22.50. (F)

SPECIAL PURPOSE PLANE, all
metal; resembles a coachmaker's
tool for an inside curve. $35.00. (F)

WOODEN WHEEL being restored with original and new parts in a blacksmith shop.

WAGON WHEEL HUBS, hickory, iron axle throats and bands. $45.00 each. 'As is' var. More refinished. (F)

WHEELWRIGHTS'
MALLETS, $19.00
each.

MORTISING GAUGE,
cherry with brass.
$65.00. (F)

TRAVELERS, eigh-
teenth century. Iron.
$125.00.

SHEET TIN, worn
edges aside from
counting groove.
$95.00+.

TRAVELERS measured the outside diameter of a wooden wheel and then measured the length of the tire to be fitted.

WHEEL REPAIR STAND, uncommon. Carried in wagons for trail repairs; center laid atop wood spindle of iron stand held wheel in horizontal position. $125.00+ set. (F Wheel)

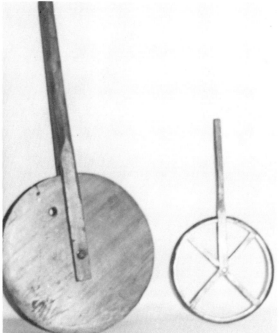

TRAVELERS (Wheel Traces), hole in wood to "eye" revolutions. Iron. $55.00 var. Wood. $95.00 var.

CARRIAGE JACK, oak, iron teeth; lifted axle for repairs. $100.00+.

COACH JACK, hickory, iron joiners. $110.00+.

WAGON JACK, New England origin; wood and iron; sliding grip; uncommon. $125.00.

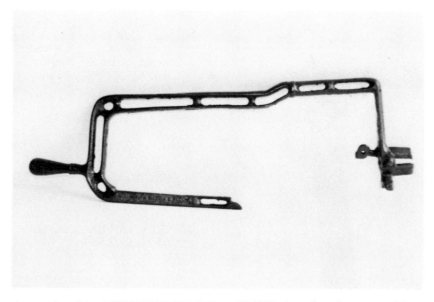

Owner thought a LIGHT BUGGY AXLE SUPPORT when changing or repairing a wheel? $28.00. (F)

BRICKLAYERS, SLATERS, AND STONEMASONS

BRICKS, very wide and very narrow, handfashioned more than a hundred years ago from clay pressed into crude wooden molds; mortar has been assimilated through age into the porous bricks.

BRICKLAYER'S HAMMER, $18.00. (F) (Iron wedge, $2.50.)

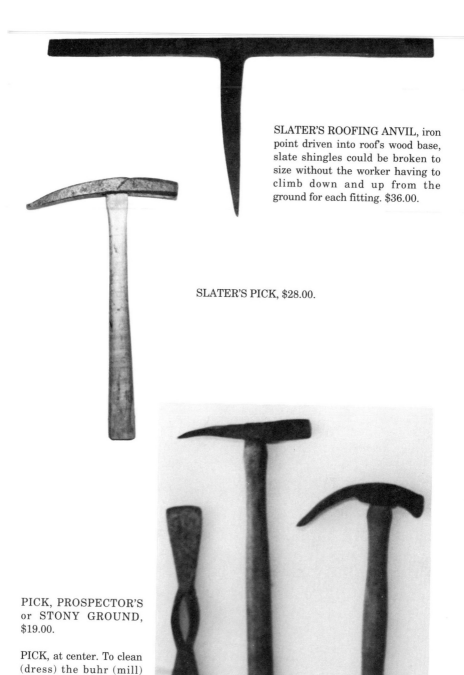

SLATER'S ROOFING ANVIL, iron point driven into roof's wood base, slate shingles could be broken to size without the worker having to climb down and up from the ground for each fitting. $36.00.

SLATER'S PICK, $28.00.

PICK, PROSPECTOR'S or STONY GROUND, $19.00.

PICK, at center. To clean (dress) the buhr (mill) stones. $20.00.

Double head CULTIVAT-ING PICK, $19.00.

STONECUTTER'S MALLET, eighteenth century. One worn side attests to hitting habit of a single owner; slashpegged handle in burl wood. $95.00+.

STONEMASON'S TRIMMING AXE, for use on sandstone. $68.00+.

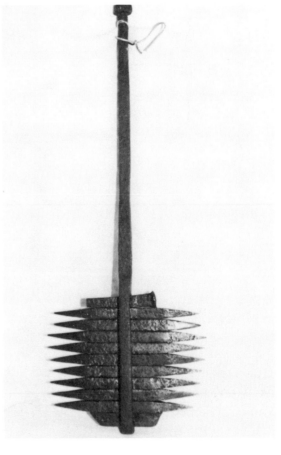

LOGGERS, RIVER LUMBERMEN

Many of these axes also used by other woodworkers.

FELLING AXE HEAD, 1812. $75.00.

GERMANIC TYPE FELLING AXE HEAD, seventeenth–eighteenth centuries. $75.00. Could also have been used for splitting.

FELLING AXE, Kelly handmade one piece iron folded at center forming handle eye terminating in sharp hammer-welded blade edge. $95.00+.

GOOSEWING BROADAXE, Eighteenth century. Northern Pennsylvania Germanic type, touchmarks. $475.00+.

Regionally a "BUZZARD'S WING" BROADAXE. $95.00.

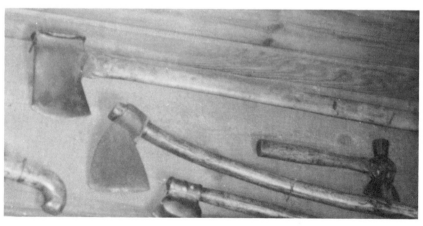

FELLING AXE with top folded hammering poll MASTMAKER'S AXE. SHIPBUILDER'S AXE, SHINGLING HATCHET at side. $75.00–95.00+.

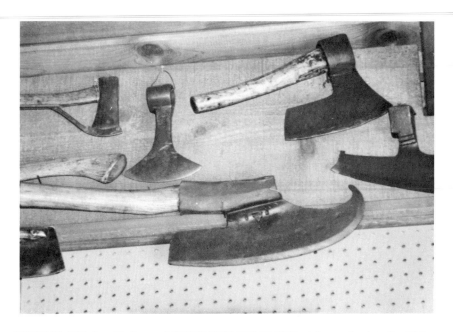

FELLING AXE, iron bladeguard. PIONEER'S AXE BLADE, style goes back to the Middle Ages. Three GOOSEWING BROADAXES, lower curved has touchmark; origin unknown. $125.00–525.00+ var.

HAND ADZE at side FELLING AXE, TRADE AXE, 'BEARDED' AXES, trimming, hewing. $95.00–150.00+.

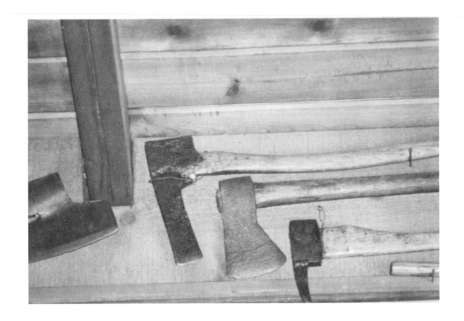

CARPENTER'S SHAPER at side. Eighteenth century MORTISE or POSTHOLE AXE, FELLING AXE, 1600–1700's. Pennsylvania. LOGGER'S POINTED PICKAROON. $100.00–125.00+. (F)

Oak GLUT, $7.50.

GLUT, very large;
iron band; oak.
$16.00.

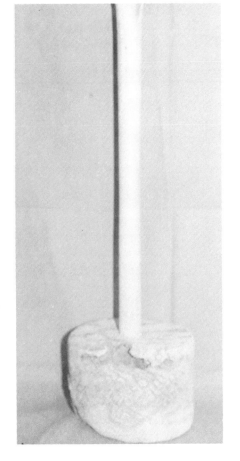

BURL MAUL, eighteenth century;
white oak handle; struck iron wedges
and oak gluts for splitting logs into
rails, etc. $68.00+.

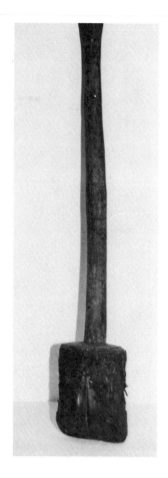

MAUL, one-piece hickory; some bark left. $14.50.

"DEBARKING" (peeling) CHISEL, 1850. For cleaning logs and removing bark for cedar posts. $95.00. (F)

IRON WEDGES, came in many sizes. $7.00–10.00.

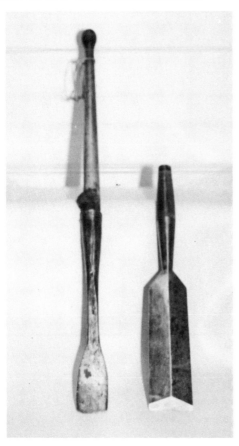

PEELING CHISEL, early 1800's. One-piece wrapped top iron; rawhide plug tightened loosened handle. $95.00+.

SLICK, shoulder pressure, both hands, as a plane; short wood handle socketed into iron; curved edge toward the bevel; a paring chisel for mortise and tenon cutting, for example. $75.00. (F)

BARKING SPUD, 1800. Spoon type, peeled bark most easily in April and May readying wood for broadaxe work; shortened lumber drying time; original handle. $125.00.

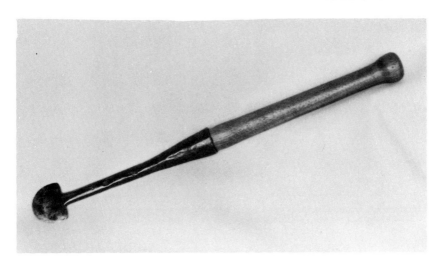

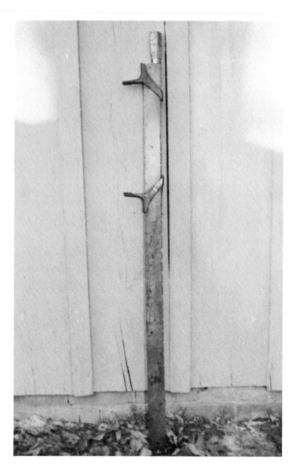

GLUE CLAMP, iron and wood; serrated edge one side held firm; for edge gluing narrow boards together making wider ones; screw top turned for pressure. $45.00. (F)

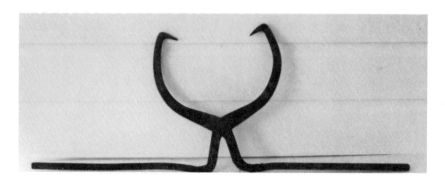

4-MEN LOG TONGS, all iron; two men each side. $45.00.

4-MEN TONGS with wood handles. $45.00.

CHAINED TONGS, $45.00.
CHAINED SPIKES, shackled logs together for river rafting. $28.00.

LOG ROLLER, $18.00.
CANT HOOK, $32.00.
Both to flip over and roll logs;
spear also an ice pusher.

LOG MARKERS, for owner's
identification (usually initials). $45.00–75.00.

SPIRAL AUGER, bored bigger holes in ships and larger buildings. $45.00.

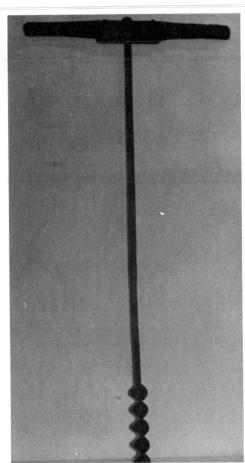

LOG MEASURE, brass and wood; to measure length and diameter, then read scale to have board feet in a log. $115.00. (F)

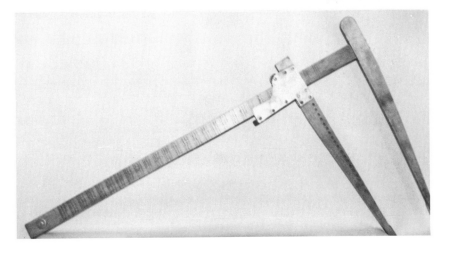

TANNERS, CURRIERS, LEATHERWORKERS

The tanner chemically treated fresh hides which after dry-stretching were passed on to the currier who worked them with tools into leather. Many early farmers tanned hides, made harness straps, hinges, and repaired boots and shoes.

CURRIER'S SLICKER, $22.00.

TANNER'S STRETCHING BOARD, this one for small game hides. $19.00.

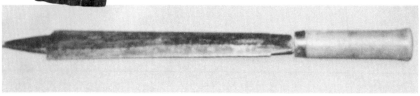

CURRIER'S SHAVING KNIFE, $58.00. (F)

STITCHING HORSE, 1840.
Hickory, for harness making and repairs; vise mortised into seat regulated by wide wood screw. (Scarce)
$225.00 var. Extra VISE underneath. $21.00.

STITCHING HORSE, hickory.
Used in both leather shops and on farms. (Now scarce)
$225.00 var.

LEATHERCUTTING KNIFE, $12.00.

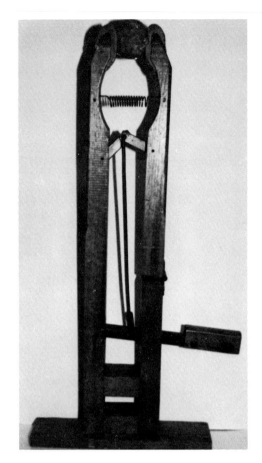

BASEBALL STITCHING VISE, ball held in locking lever controlled pincers. $75.00. (F)

COBBLER'S AWL, thumb screw allowed varied-size points. $18.00. (F)

COBBLER'S TOOLS, $75.00 var., set of seven. (F)

BENCH, 1790–1800. Cobbler made; pedestal holds iron shoelast post. $495.00.

COBBLER'S STAND & LASTS, 1890. Iron base, lasts fit over pointed wood post. $95.00+ set. (F)

BOOTSTRETCHERS, maple, three parts grooved to be fitted together, divided into required size. $45.00 comp.

BOOTLASTS, preferred chestnut; to hold parts when putting on soles and heels with woodpegs; lasts heavily usage marked with small holes. $12.00–26.00.

COBBLER'S SOLES CUTTER, $29.00. (F)
Sharp base-edge iron struck with iron MALLET
having leather roll side insertions. $35.00. (F)

DOUBLE SHOELAST, $25.00. (F)
COBBLER'S HAMMER, $19.00. (F)

TINNERS

As his affluence and towns grew the tinner set up his shop where before he had traveled afoot with backpack tools, on mule/horseback, and then in a wagon, repairing pots and pans and making other light metal essentials. Two views of a TINNER'S SHOP ANVIL (with a massively heavy "Buffalo Head" SWAGE BLACK on the log stump for making heavy forgings by hand).

TINNER'S ANVIL,
$95.00 var.

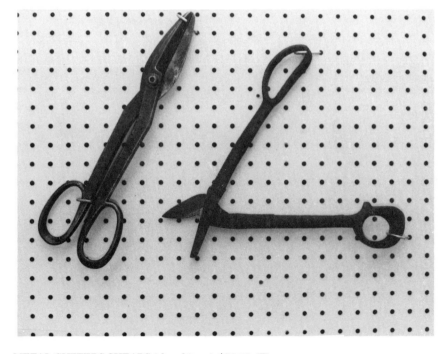

METAL CUTTERS SHEARS (closed jaws). $22.50. (F)
OPEN JAWS, rare. Cut an easier straight line. $25.00.

WOODWORKERS

It would be inaccurate to state that all tools, other than those already universally recognized as having been made to a single purpose for a specific type of craftsman, as the cooper's croze and the smith's bolt header, are so restricted. Too many overlap through their varied uses by various users. The axe, for example, for so long our only diversified implement, which is shown herein first as a woodworker's raising tool, to build. There were few boundaries beyond suitability in the days when there were too few tools for far too many chores among our American pioneers.

GOOSEWING BROADAXE, eighteenth century. Northern Pennsylvania Germanic; touchmarks American poll. $525.00+.

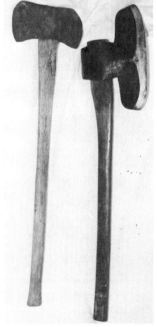

YANKEE AXE, double head. 1850. $75.00. BROADAXE, sharpened one side. $125.00+.

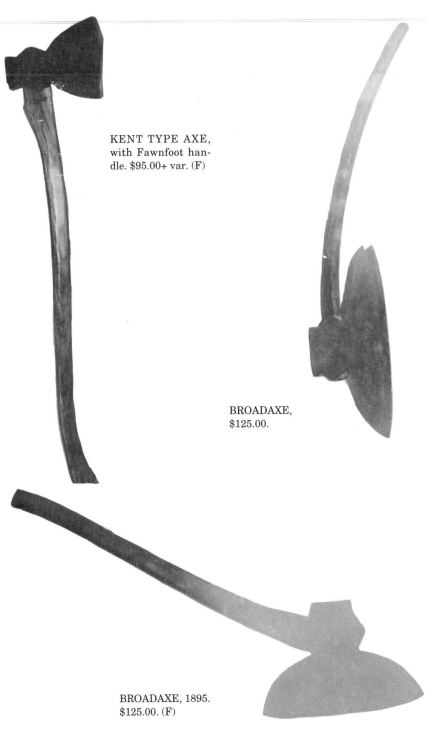

KENT TYPE AXE, with Fawnfoot handle. $95.00+ var. (F)

BROADAXE, $125.00.

BROADAXE, 1895. $125.00. (F)

FOOT ADZE HEAD, $25.00.
AMERICAN ADZE HEAD, dated 1792. $95.00+.

CARPENTER'S MALLET, $10.50.

CARPENTER'S SHAKERS
MALLET/HAMMER, solid walnut
block, heavily nicked one side shows
one owner. $135.00.

PLOW PLANE, 1850–1860. Maker marked. Adjustable, cherry with brass fittings; made a groove (plowed) the boards for joining; usually had a set of eight irons (blades) in various widths. $150.00+ var.

TONGUE & GROOVE PLANES, initialed, maple; one early use was on fine seventeenth century butterfly and gateleg tables. $125.00–150.00 var.

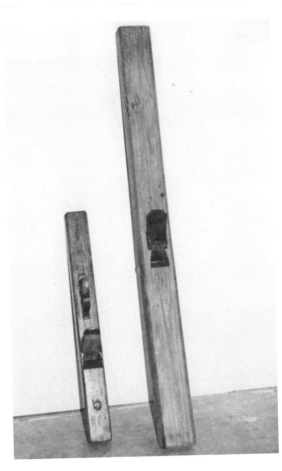

COOPER'S LONG JOINT-ER, (barrel maker). Almost 6'. $175.00. (F)

SHORTER JOINTER, $55.00. (F)

SHORTER JOINTER used as a SHIWRIGHT'S PLANE, $65.00. (F)

MOULDING PLANE, cherry, made a bead. (F) RABBET PLANE, maple, corner grooving. Last two $45.00 var. (F)

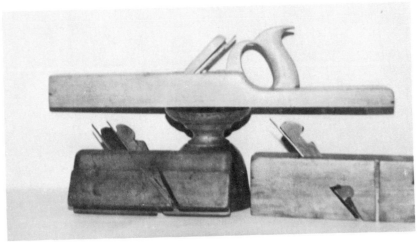

CARPENTER'S LONG
JOINTER or FLOOR
PLANE, maple, about
36". $85.00. (F)

SHORTER JOINTER
(TRYING) PLANE,
maple, approx. 24".
$75.00. (F)

HORNED RABBET
SMOOTHING, $75.00
var. (F)

RABBET, cherry,
notched to fit wood,
earliest had the widest
'eyes'. $65.00 var. (F)

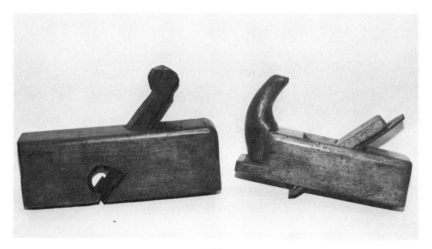

MOULDING PLANES, maple. $40.00 each. (F)

RABBET PLANE, maple, wide 'eye.' $65.00 var.
HOLLOW PLANE, maple. $45.00 var. (F)

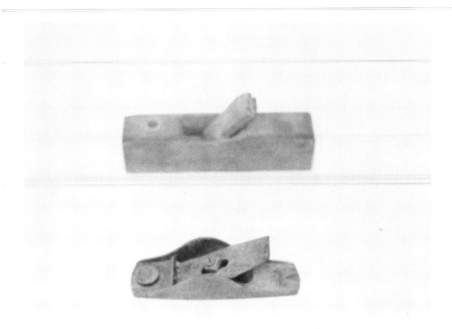

BENCH/SMOOTHING PLANE, metal, dating into the 1900's. $25.00 up. (F)
SMOOTHING/BLOCK PLANE, $35.00. Both for small cabinetwork, miniature size.

JACK (Smoothing) PLANE, $37.50 var.

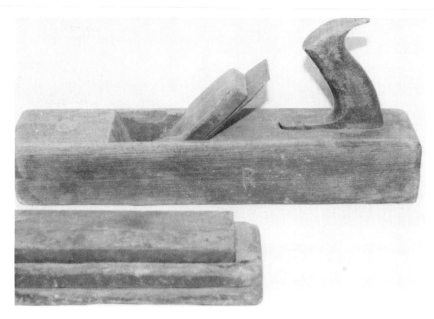

BENCH PLANE, $45.00.
OILSTONE in wood box. $75.00.

WITCHET, 1840. Combined hardwoods, brass lined throat, double blades, a turning plane to smooth poles. $225.00+. (F)

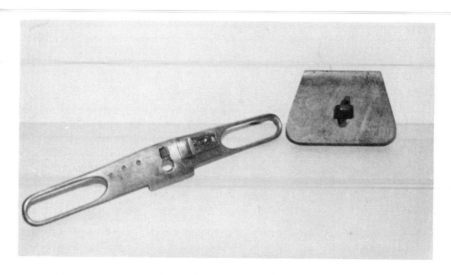

WHEELWRIGHT'S ROUTER, he quickly made when he needed such a simple routing (scooping) device to level the bottom of a groove or recess. $45.00.
PATTERNMAKER'S SCRAPER PLANE, brass, for delicate work. $75.00. (F)

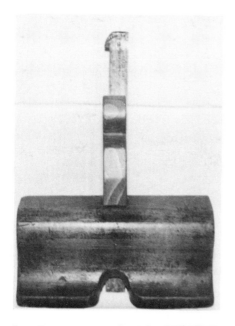

American factory made style of ROUTER begun in England where it was humorously termed 'OLD WOMAN'S TOOTH' as its single iron looked like a snaggle. $75.00.

ROUTER, carved out handle. $45.00.

SHOP ADVERTISING SIGN, all original as made by owner, wood, and metal. $350.00+.

SAW GAUGE, center determined depth of tooth for sharpening. $20.00. (F)
SAW TOOTH BENDING TOOL, determined the width of the cuts, necessary tools in sharpening the steel sawteeth with a file to assure uniformity. $22.00. (F)

RIP SAWS
Smallest #5 — '5-point'
Center #8 — '8-point'
Last #10 — finishing
$20.00–35.00. (F)

MITER SAW,
reversible cutting
edges. $12.50 var. (F)

KEYHOLES SAW,
$12.50 var. (F)

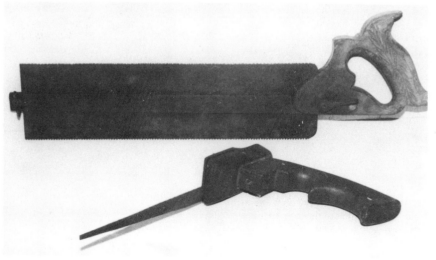

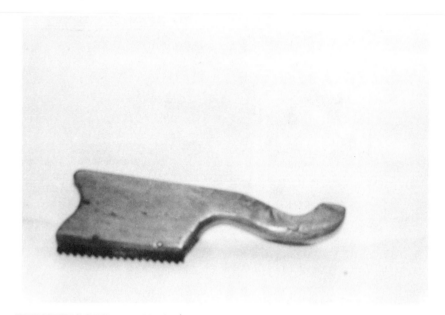

TRENCHING SAW, 1840. Maple. $85.00.

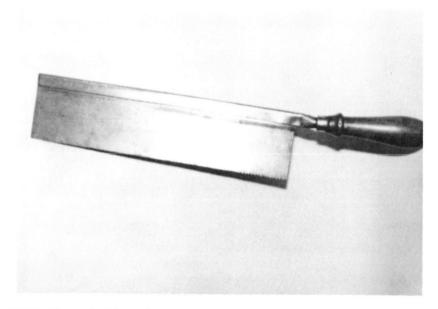

BUHL (Fine-toothed fret) SAW, signed, cherry
handle, ornamental lines, forerunner of hand
jigsaw or scroll. $85.00. (F)

CHAIRMAKER'S FRAME SAW, (Felloe or Turning) about 30" with ½" wide blade. $45.00.

BUCKSAW, rigid blade; used by woodsmen and at home for sawing fireplace and cook-stove lengths. $10.00–22.00. (F)

TAP AND DIE (AUGER), 1850's. To cut wood threads for early vises, side rails of beds, and so on. $145.00. (F)

SPIRAL AUGER, $35.00. (F)

CABINETMAKER'S HAND SANDER, maple, handle folds for toolbox storage. $35.00.

OILSTONE, walnut box with lid. $95.00+.

SCREWDRIVERS, $6.00–10.00. (F)

One of our earliest tools, there must be more old DRAWKNIVES still around than any other antique implement. In Pennsylvania it was the "Snitzel-Knife," drawn toward the user, and increasing even faster with the appearance of the Snitzelbank or Shaving Horse where the worker could sit for work on its extended bench or a separate stool. Drawknives shaped and rounded stock for general usage, as axe and other tool handles, yokes, and on and on, their finishes often final-smoothed with scrapers and shavers.

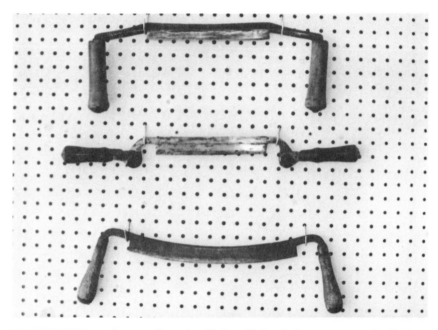

DRAWKNIVES, top has an 8" cutting blade with hand clearance on each side in a reverse curve; tangs extend through handles, bent over to prevent handles slipping off. Center (F) has adjustable handles. Lower used by a Carriagemaker. $35.00–38.00.

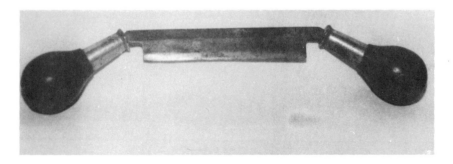

CABINETMAKER'S DRAWKNIFE, $25.00–40.00. (F)

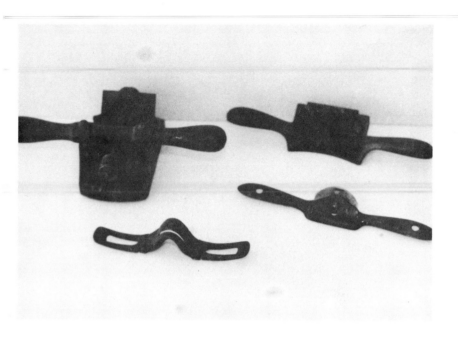

All metal SHAVERS, THREE SPOKESHAVES and the largest a Cooper's DOWN-SHAVE, metal shavers evolving about 1850–60. $22.00–35.00. (F)

RULES, wood, brass fixtures, four-fold. $38.00–50.00 (ea). (F)

RULE, wood. $22.50.

TRY SQUARES, cherry, polished iron, brass bound and inlays. $25.00–45.00. (F)

SET TRY SQUARE, cherry, polished iron, brass bound blade at a fixed angle saved time in constantly having to reset. $47.50. (F)

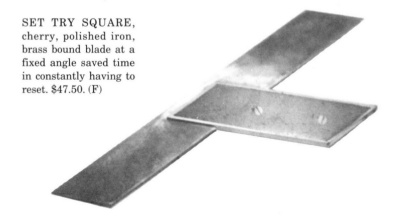

CABINETMAKERS' ADJUSTABLE SQUARES, for fixed 45 degree angles; last for semi-circles; can be adjusted to odd angles; rosewood. $35.00–45.00 ea. (F)

Steel SQUARES, $12.00–14.00. (F)

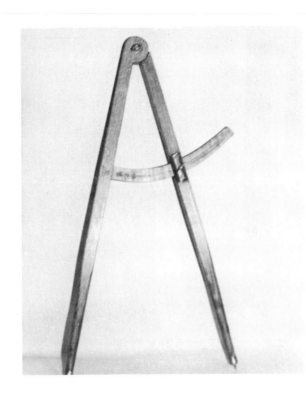

DIVIDER, pearwood, brass fittings and wingtips; this larger size much used in carriage making. $45.00. (F)

DIVIDERS, all metal, shorter has adjustable wingnut; used by all woodworkers for measuring and scribing. $45.00. (F)

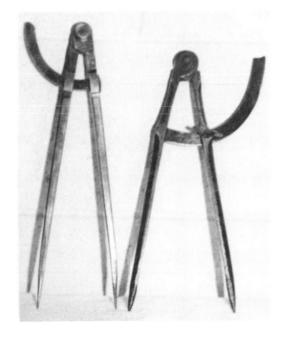

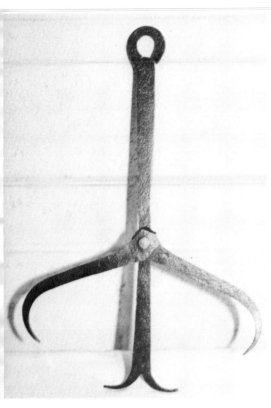

While regarded as metalworking tools CALIPERS are also important to wood-turners, patternmakers, anyone measuring wood thicknesses.

DOUBLE CALIPERS, for use on a lathe with the stock in motion. $95.00+.

CALIPERS, iron with brass joiner. $31.50.

DOUBLE CALIPERS, $48.00. (F)
4-SECTION , $55.00. (F)

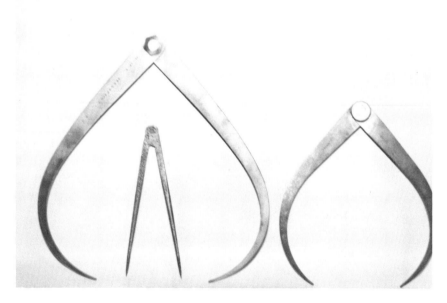

CALIPERS, $19.00. (F)
DIVIDERS, iron. $12.50.

SLITTING GAUGE, cherry; thinly cut wide widths for drawer bottoms, etc. when too difficult using other tools. $75.00. (F)

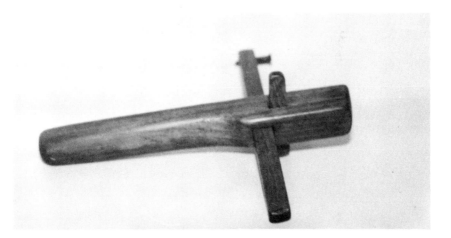

MARKING GAUGE, special purpose; note horseshoe nail for scribing marks. $75.00.

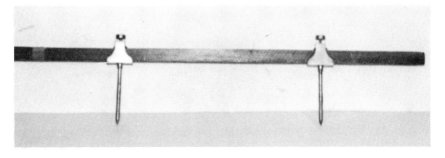

TRAMMEL, 1890. Wood and brass; mechanical drawing tool for scribing ovals. $98.00. (F)

LEVELS, $79.00–110.00. (F)
TOP, initialed rosewood, brass bound; pat. dated 1872.
CENTER, cherry, brass bound; pat. dated 1890.
SMALLEST, cherry, brass throat; pat. dated 1867.

CHALK LINE REEL, eighteenth century. Mortised, well balanced hickory, freely spins. $110.00.

TWO PLUMB BOBS, both brass, one with leather case. $40.00–75.00. (F)

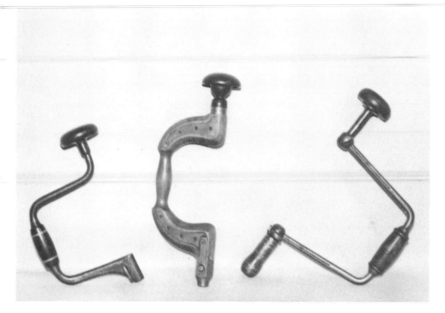

CABINETMAKERS' BITSTOCKS, early metal split socket device. (F)
CENTER, 1840, quarter plated brass on rosewood, button release catch.
ADJUSTABLE JAW BIT, 1840–45. Knurled knob chuck control for bit.
$75.00–260.00. (F)

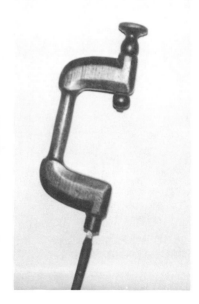

BITSTOCK, one of the first American to have
a socket catch holding bit in place; stem knob
turned with head, knob pushed through and
glued into stockhead. $175.00+.

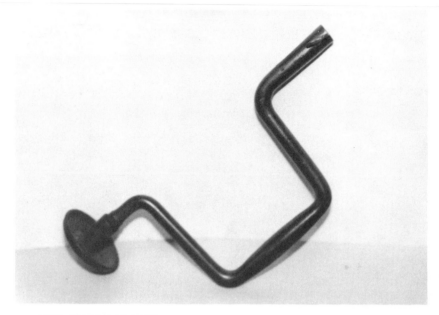

COACHMAKER'S BITSTOCK, 1845–50. Metal, thumblatch quickly released bit, larger than many-head, rested against the worker's chest. $65.00 var. (F)

CORNER BRACE, metal with wood fixtures. $85.00. (F)

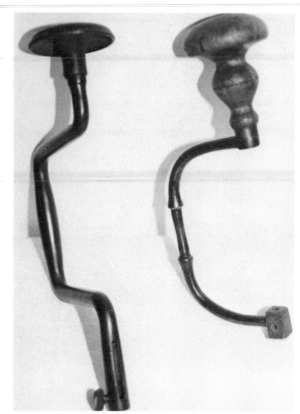

BITSTOCK, all metal with set screw to hold bit, for narrow pattern-making. $75.00. (F)

BITSTOCK (BRACE), 1850. Revolving hand-grip, wood head, metal chunk held bit locked in with a wedge. $95.00. (F)

BITSTOCK, all metal; split socket form but metal chuck to hold bit firm; in fairly good sup-ply. $45.00. (F)

BARREL BUNG AUGER, $45.00. (F)
SCREWDRIVERS, $18.00 var. (F)
REAMER, $58.00.
RAFT AUGER, $65.00. (F)
BORE AUGER, $35.00. (F)
CORNER BRACE, $85.00. (F)

REAMER, for enlarging holes as in hubs and pump logs. $45.00.
TAP AUGER, $35.00.

CORNER CHISELS, two cutting edges at right angles to square up mortise corners; hit with a wood mallet; top is eighteenth century; these among our earliest construction tools. $95.00+.

GOUGE, seventeenth century. All metal; a round chisel making a circular sweep. $125.00–150.00+.

SKEW CHISEL, one side only ground to a bevel; brass ferrule; there were lefts and rights. $35.00.

FORMING CHISELS, $45.00–55.00 (ea).

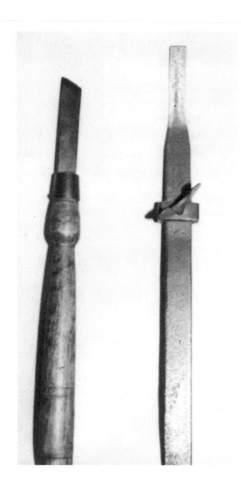

GOUGE, seventeenth century; wingnut depth set for chaneling and roughing out wood; used on a turning lathe. $95.00.

FORMING CHISEL, $45.00.

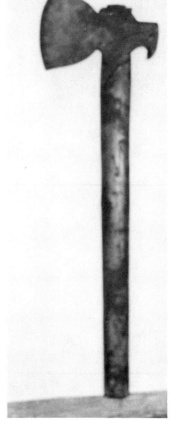

HATCHET, 1845. Earliest factorymade type. $45.00.

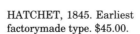

HATCHET
1845
Earliest factorymade type $19.00

CARPENTER'S PLAIN EYE BRAD (or Tack) HAMMER , $18.00.(F)
LATHING HATCHET, flat side prevented marring ceiling in such close hammering. $22.50. (F)
CARPENTER'S CLAW HAMMER, $15.00. (F)

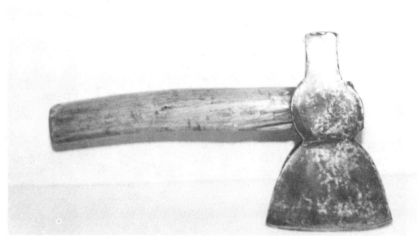

SHINGLING HATCHET, forerunner of today's household hatchet. $35.00. (F)

There were wet coopers who made barrels and casks for liquids and dry coopers who made them for sugar and meals. The white cooper made both except in smaller units such as canteens, rum and powder kegs. We've read John Allen boarded the Mayflower as a cooper; it is recorded such craftsmen ranked with privileged status on long voyages of whalers needing wooden containers for oil and that coopering predates 100 A.D.

COOPER'S HAND ADZE (Colt's Foot), equal weight on both sides of handle; adze to shape staves; a hammer to drive hoops into place. $55.00+.

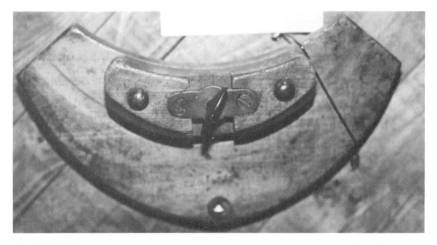

The HOWELL, having a small blade and a semi-circular fence, smoothed both barrel ends so a uniform CROZE cut could be made to easily insert barrel heads. $145.00+ var.

Top and side view of a CROZE.
$175.00+ var.

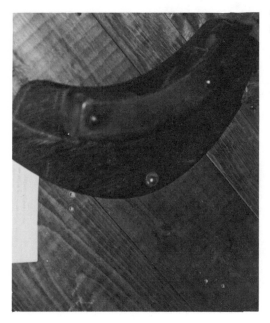

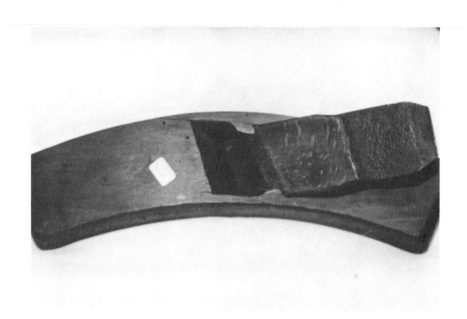

COOPER'S SUNPLANE, to level barreltop staves. $125.00+.

COOPER'S CROZE, entirely brass riveted to wood; cut a shallow groove to fit in a barrel top or bottom round. $175.00+. (Rear box a prop.)

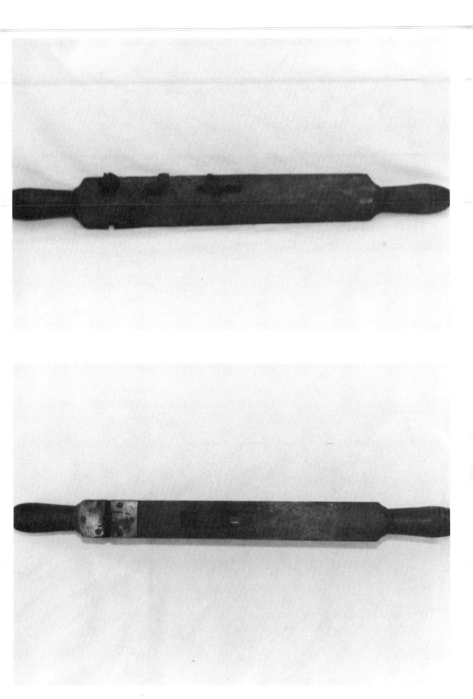

Upper and lower sides of a rare COOPER'S BARRELTOP PLANE & MARKING GAUGE, $150.00+.

COOPER'S PULL
SCRAPER, maple
handle, brass fer-
rule. $45.00.

COOPER'S HAND ADZE, $40.00.
WOOD CLAMP, $25.00. (F)

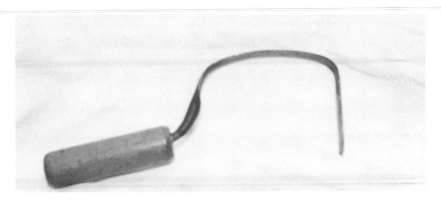

COOPER'S WOOD SCRAPER, extra sharp blade. $45.00.

JOINTER PLANE
This cooper's tool was the heaviest of all jointers. Used upturned at an angle with two legs holding one end up about 18" off the floor, the staves were pushed along the two blades while the plane itself remained stationary, forming a bevel along the sides of the staves' edges. $195.00 var.

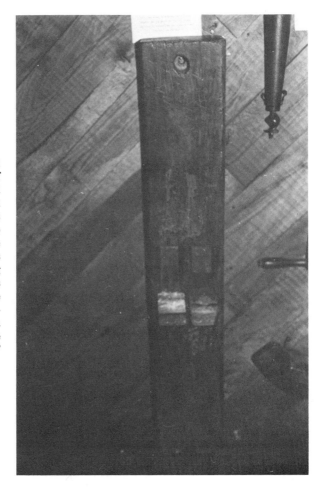

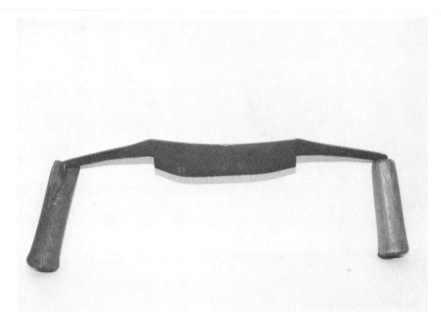

COOPER'S DRAWKNIFE, tines through and bent over at handle ends for added strength. $45.00.

COOPER'S DRAWKNIFE, $125.00 var.

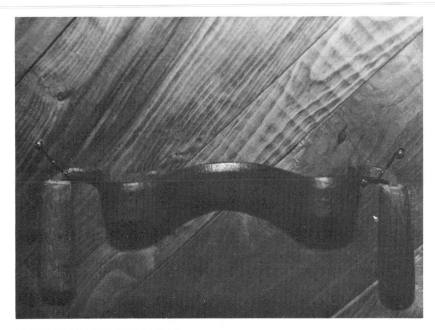

COOPER'S DRAWKNIFE, $145.00.

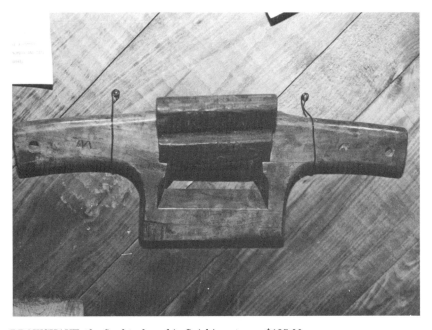

DRAWSHAVE, the final tool used in finishing staves. $125.00.

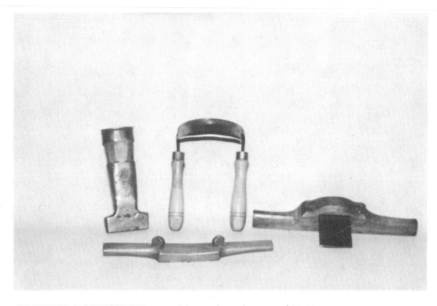

COOPER'S DOWNSHAVE, as making on barrel staves. $75.00+.
DRAWSHAVE, center, final finishing staves. $75.00. (F)
HOOPSETTER, touchmark initials, base groove, 1800. $125.00.
LITTLE SPOKESHAVE, adjustable tang blade cherry and brass, wheelwright's. $40.00. (F)

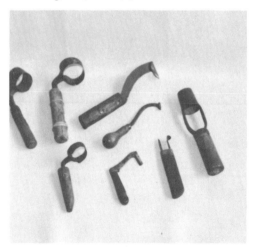

COOPER'S RACE KNIVES,
(Wood Marking Tools) (F)
BOWLMAKER'S CLOSED SCORPERS (Round
Shaves), for preliminary finishing of woods.

All salesmen's samples, rare. $150.00–195.00+ (ea).

BOWLMAKER'S ROUND
CLOSED SHAVER, (Scorper).
About 3" dia. $85.00.

Four CHAMFERING KNIVES that cut the Chime (Chimb) — the rim staves of a barrel or cask. $75.00–150.00.

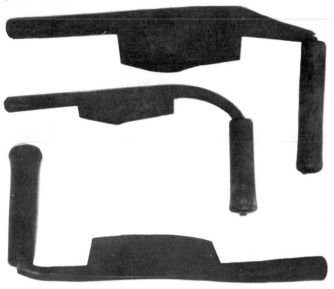

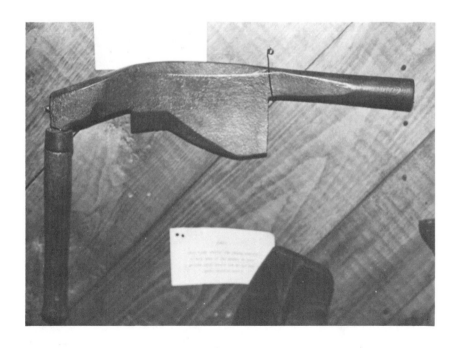

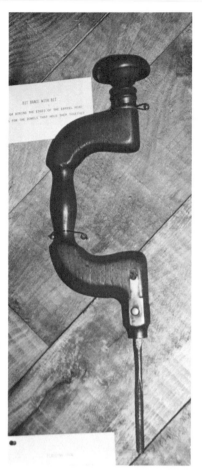

COOPER'S BIT BRACE & BIT, brass on wood; for boring edges of wood strips used for barrel heads — for dowell inserts that held them together. $200.00+.

HEAD FLOAT, 1832. Maker: D.B. Barton, Rochester, N.Y. Smoothed barrel heads. $145.00+.

"NANTUCKET PATTERN" HOOP DRIVER & HAMMER, with one end could directly hammer hoops into position; or, fitting its other grooved edge to the wood, the hoop could be set using a second striking hammer. $95.00. (F)

HOOPSETTER, concave base, all wood; struck with a hoop hammer. $52.00.

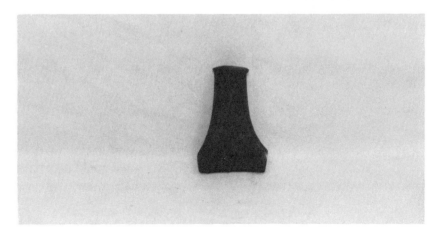

COOPER'S HOOP DRIVER, held on a barrel and struck with a hammer to drive hoops into position. $145.00+.

BARREL HOOK, used to lift barrel into position by catching the hook in the Chime — or Chimb — the rim. $45.00.

COOPER'S BECK IRON, steel faced iron anvil to splay and rivet hoops. $125.00+.

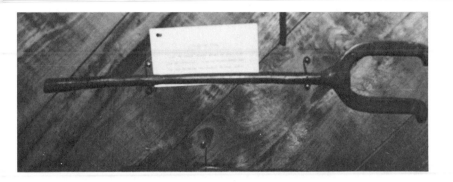

FLAGGING IRON, forced the joints apart so flags could be inserted. $150.00.

BUNG PICK, removed wooden bungs; if the bung split the end hook could be used to lift out the pieces. Maker marked with pat. dates. 1879–80. $145.00+.

CHIMING IRON, forced the flags or rushes into the cask or barrel joints to prevent leakage. $125.00+.

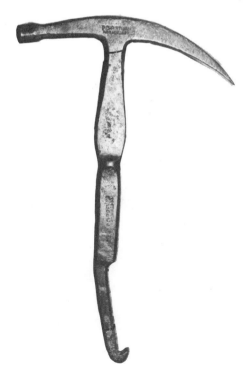

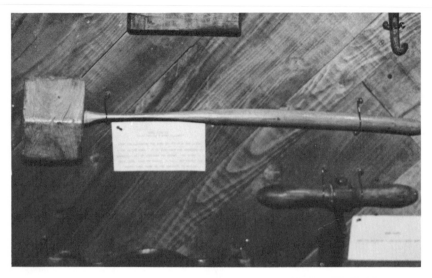

BUNG STARTER, maple; loosened by hitting stave closest to the bung; also used for 'sounding out' barrels; upon striking if there was a dull thud it meant full; a ringing response denoted only partial contents. $95.00+.

COOPER'S BURNING IRONS

JAN and CORN, to identify distillery grain type containers and month. $175.00+ set.

Burned labels on heads of casks and barrels; today this is done with brass stencils. $175.00 set.

COOPER'S STENCIL WHEEL, for dating and numbering barrel heads. $165.00+.

STENCIL, brass, owner marked with complete information. $125.00+ var.

COOPER'S MARKING HAMMER/NUMBERING WHEEL, to place serial number and date on every barrel head. $195.00 var.

FARMS

FROWS were faster than saws for splitting (riving) shingles, half-round hoops, shakes, and clapboards; with sharp bladesides on wood to be rived with handle in up position the top of the iron was hit with a wood mallet, and with a twist of the wrist, the object snapped off its larger wood piece. These three FROWS are particularly handsome, the slimmest least plentiful and popular in riving tobacco stakes for curing plants; the center was frugally made from a file the smith had first made and worn out in another usage; the last is well wrapped; all handles are slashpegged at the eye for minimal loosening.

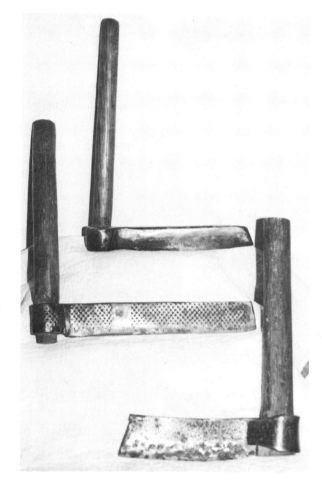

FROWS, $45.00+ (ea).

FROW, made at a farm forge, crude but effective. $45.00.

FROW MALLET, hardwood, somewhat large and awkward for this work but looks well used. $12.50.

BURL FROW MALLET, $65.00.

CARPENTER'S MALLET, wide iron bands each end. $25.00.

LAND MEASURE (TRAVELER), center loud wood clacker counted by rods each full turn of the 38" dia. wheel pushed by the upper handle, all wood, center pin. $125.00–150.00.

WEEDCUTTER, $12.00.
POSTHOLE STARTER, (seems to me it could double as a fence stretcher.) $7.50.

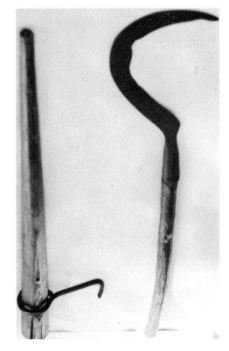

FENCE STRETCHER, rapidly homemade with a serrated step for holding the wire. $9.00.

GRINDSTONE, $55.00 var.

(BARN BEAM) BORING RIG, worker sat on rear of two-handled drill base, turning with both hands to lower the bit, cutting two round holes that made mortise hand-chiseling simpler. $65.00. (F)

CENTER BIT, only cut downward; turned shelf at right cutter edge pulled shavings up; used with a brace. $9.00. (F)
GINSENG HOE, to loosen ground around and dig roots for sale to apothecaries, another cash source on early farms. $45.00.

SPADE DRAG, all wood; approx. 7' long handle attached Drag to cultivator to prevent dirt covering newly sprouted plants. $45.00.
FIELD FORK/HOE, special purpose. $38.00.

COLTER PLOW, the Colter is the plowshare to cut turf. $48.00.

Two HARROWS performing the same purpose, to break up clods of dirt with the big iron spikes that protruded underneath in preparing the fields for planting; man-pushed, mule-pulled. $48.00 each var.

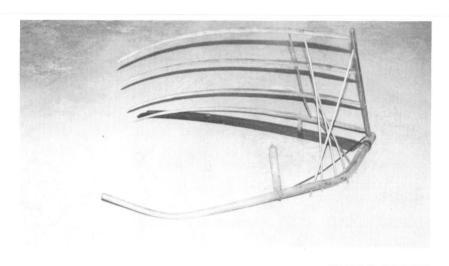

CRADLE SCYTHE, four-finger bow; one-nib, handhold, indicates earliest; metal blade. $175.00+.

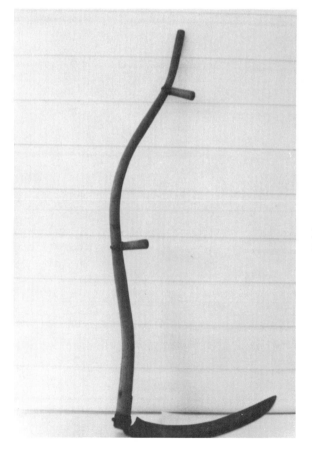

MOWING SCYTHE, $75.00+.

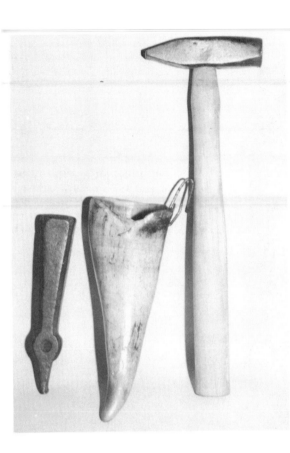

DENGELSHTOCK, iron anvil for sharpening scythes with CARRYING CASE, carved natural animal's horn.
PICK, to clean field implements. $175.00 the set.

SCYTHE STONE CARRIER, seventeenth century carved from one piece wood. $110.00+.
OILSTONE, walnut box. $75.00.

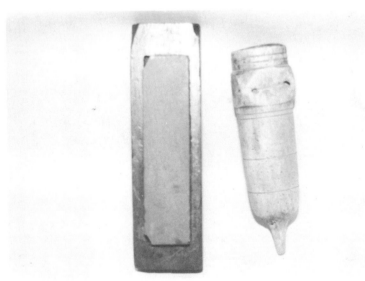

GRUBBING HOES/CHOPPERS, an extension riveted onto the eye of a single blade for deeper digging to make holes for planting or to penetrate rockier ground. $35.00 ea.

Steel forged onto the iron blade end for greater strength and less frequent sharpening. $39.00.

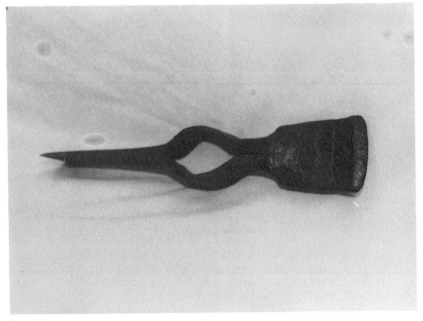

FIELD HOES/CHOPPERS, handles made to worker's needs, the larger eyes indicating greater age of the tool; center is a cotton chopper. $22.00.

FIELD KNIVES, $25.00–35.00.

FORK, eighteenth century. $165.00+.

GRAINS SHOCK STALK TYERS, fitted with binder twine and set in the center of sheaves of grain and corn stalks in a field; when shock is desired diameter, turning the Tyer binds the lot and with the Tyer lifted out, the shock stands alone; the one on top once won a prize at a harvest fair. $145.00+.

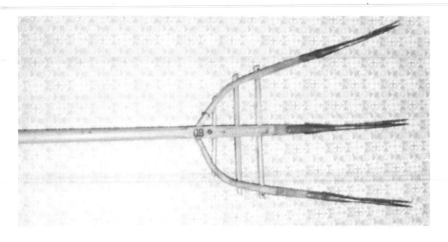

HAYFORK
Impressed maker's
initials; long metal
prongs; Pennsylva-
nia origin. $475.00.

HAYFORK, $200.00.
SPADE, turned sides
indicate a RUTTER
SPADE for cutting
drains — trenches for
water courses and/or
harvesting on our
peat lands. $48.00.

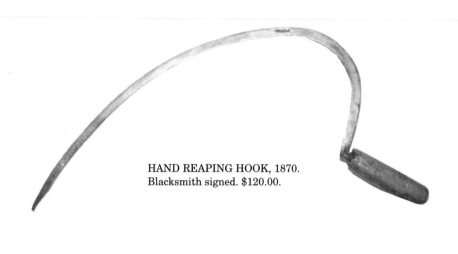

HAND REAPING HOOK, 1870.
Blacksmith signed. $120.00.

RAKE, all wood. $125.00.

GRASS/HAY CROOK, to pull clumps toward
the reaper or hay from a stack. $35.00.

TOBACCO STALKS DRYING

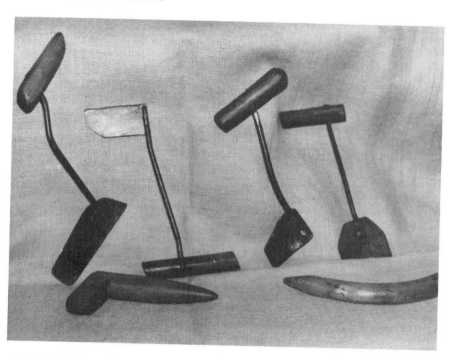

TOBACCO CUTTERS, $28.00+ (ea).
PEGS (Handplanters), applewood. $25.00+ (ea).

TOBACCO CUTTER, type usually for Burley. $45.00.

TOBACCO CART, for auction warehouse inside use only; 3" wide iron wheels would sink in soft ground; top curved to prevent piled-high tobacco 'hands' from readily slipping off. $125.00+.

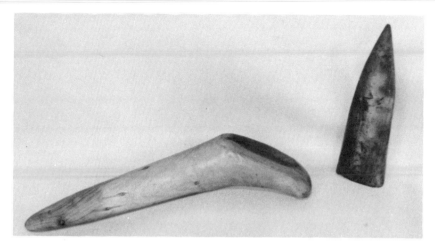

TOBACCO PEG, natural wood knuckle for stoopwork planting. $32.00.
TOBACCO SPIKE, to thread cut plants down onto stakes to dry. $18.00.

TOBACCO SPIKE,
brass. $45.00.

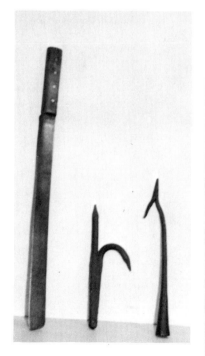

CORNCUTTING KNIFE, $25.00.
ICE PUSHER LOG ROLLER, $12.50.
HAYCROOK, $12.50.

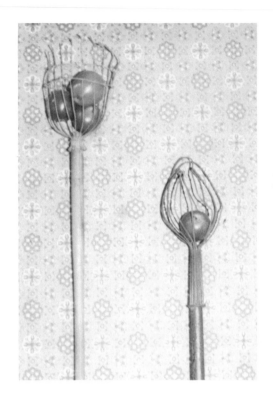

APPLE PICKERS,
$45.00+ (ea). (F)

CIDER PRESS, maker
stamped; fruit dumped
in top hopper, juice
flows below; handle
operated. $310.00. (F)

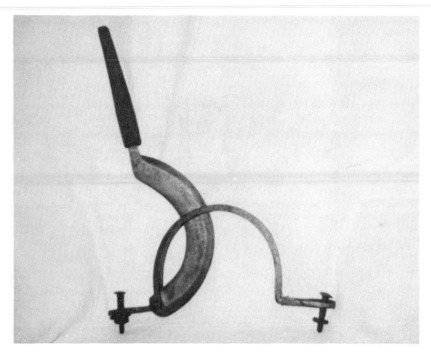

FODDER CUTTER, bolted to plank, blade pulled down on fodder stalks laid under frame cut to desired lengths. $45.00+. (F)

HAYKNIFE, sawed into stack
for any amount. $35.00. (F)

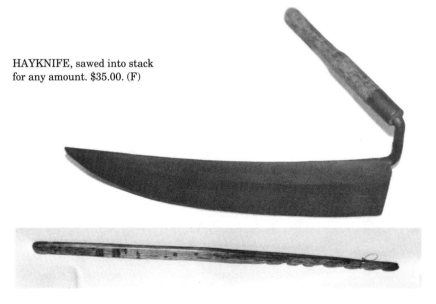

FODDER STRIPPER, one piece wood; interesting in wall decor with other tools. $22.50.

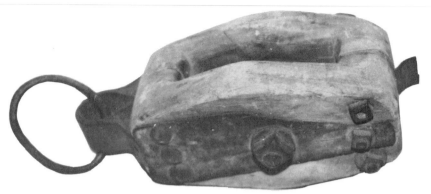

PULLEY BLOCK, this cypress with iron fixtures and wood inside wheel for the rope pulled hay up into the barnloft. $42.00.

COPPER RINGS opened by their tiny screws were put in the snout of uncooperative hogs and controlled by the PULL whose button ends were not inhumane; eye holes for ropes. $28.00 set.

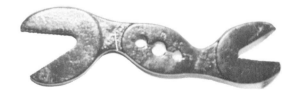

ALLIGATOR WRENCH, $45.00.

WAGON TOOLBOX, all original, wood sides, cotton waste in metal dome accommodated oilcan spout and drippings with waste cotton; "Whitely" in lacy iron ends. $175.00+.

WHEELBARROW, brackets for removable sides; maker's name; all original. $165.00+.

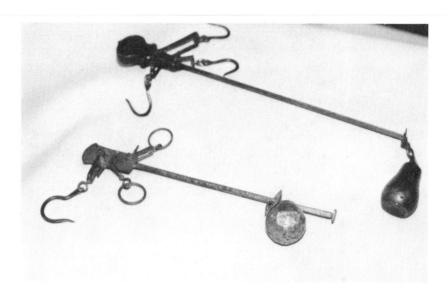

STEELYARDS (Stilyerds), iron off center balance scale with sliding weight on arm; lower is a brass arm with a thinly-cased brass iron ball weight. $35.00–45.00.

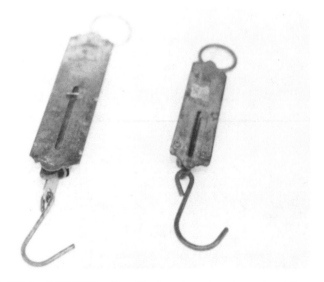

SPRING BALANCE (Chicken) SCALES, 5lb., 2lb.; hanging rings brass faced iron, manufacturer marked; (some might recall Grandma tying together the legs of squawking hens, hanging them by the strings upside down on the scales, and with feathers flying in protest the fowl was weighed for sale on the farm or at country markets). $28.00–35.00 var.

SIGN on wall outside passenger depot waiting room in the late 1800's and early 1900's. $125.00+.

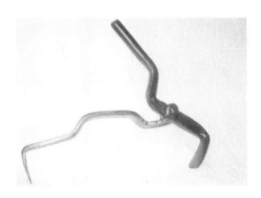

FREIGHT HANDLER'S TONGS, $35.00.

FREIGHT PLATFORM CRATE MOVER, homemade. $45.00.

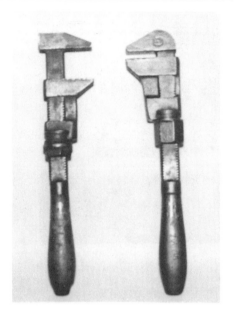

RAILROAD (Monkey) WRENCHES (F)
Imprinted: Illinois Central, $48.00+.
           Baltimore & Ohio, $48.00+.

RAILROAD BLACKSMITH'S
SPRING TONGS, pat'd. but-
ton grips on inside of jaws.
$28.00. (F)

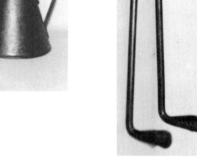

RAILROAD TORCHES, (F)
Marked: Pennsylvania $45.00+.
        Eagle $45.00+.
        Baltimore & Ohio $45.00+.

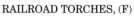

144

MATE'S HORN, 1830. Owner's name imprinted; megaphone type found at Easton River, Pennsylvania. $125.00+.

CLACKET, 1860's. Maple; teeth whirled on handle axle producing an earsplitting noise; for 'alarums'; aboard ships; said to have later been a 'WAKER' at an east coast convent. $135.00+.

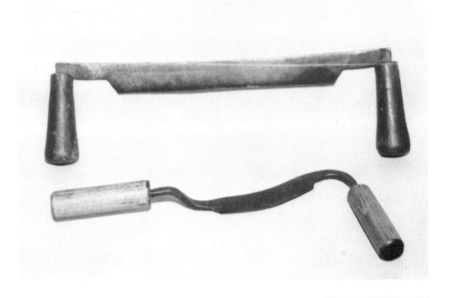

MAST DRAWKNIFE, 1830. $48.00.

SHIP'S COOPER'S DRAWKNIFE, iron blade curved for shaving staves of barrels. $45.00.

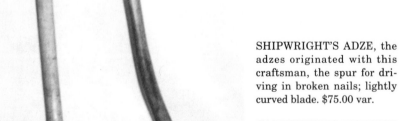

SHIPWRIGHT'S ADZE, the adzes originated with this craftsman, the spur for driving in broken nails; lightly curved blade. $75.00 var.

CARPENTER'S MORTISE AXE, head-hit as a chisel with a wood mallet (or maul); farmers as well as smiths made them. $75.00 var.

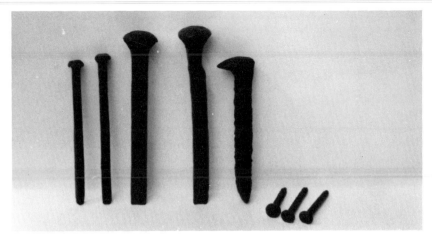

SHIP'S ROSETOP NAILS and SPIKES — FLOOR PLANK RAILROAD TIES NAILS top replacement dated. $5.00–8.00 ea.

GOUGE (Round Chisel), used on an early 1800's sailing vessel; two hands pressure, iron burned-through handle and bent over on top to firm. $90.00.

SHIPWRIGHT'S MALLET, hard maple. $45.00.

LEAD POURING LADLES, each long handled. $35.00–45.00+.

STONE CRUCIBLE, held flux for melting. $45.00.

LADLE, two-lip iron to pour molten lead. $35.00+.

LEAD POURING LADLE, $45.00.

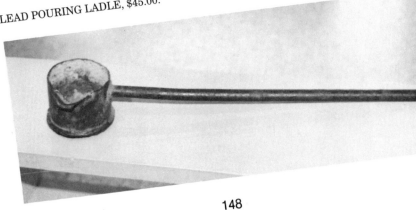

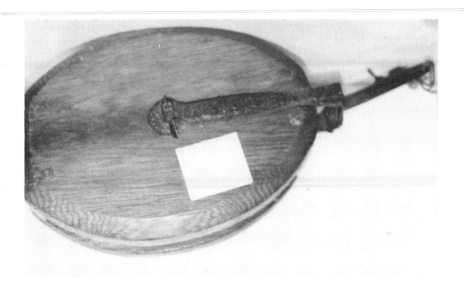

WHALE BLOCK (Rope Pulley), 1800, very large; made by ship's carpenter; cut two pieces from green oak; whalebone spreaders set between against the wood warping and splintering; ship's smith provided the ironwork (dealer's tag). $250.00+.

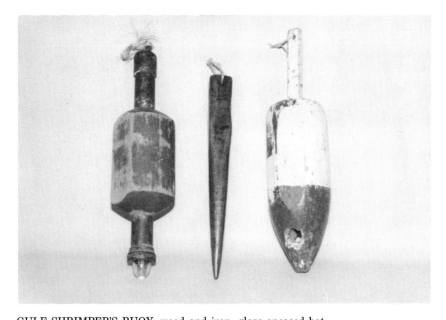

GULF SHRIMPER'S BUOY, wood and iron, glass encased battery light in top floating end to indicate net. $31.50. (F)
FID, 1860. Maple, came in many sizes; to stretch rope eyes and open strands for splicing. $28.00.
LOBSTER BUOY, Maine, rope hole. All original finishes. $17.00.

DOUBLE FLUE ARCTIC HARPOON, 1813. Forges by ship's smith for whaler's Captain; (brass plate details). $425.00+ var.

MARINER'S DIVIDERS, 1810. Brass; suitable for charting vast ocean areas; slot for marking pencil in flat side base. $125.00 var.

OYSTER SHUCKER, $10.00. (F)

INDEX

151